Visual

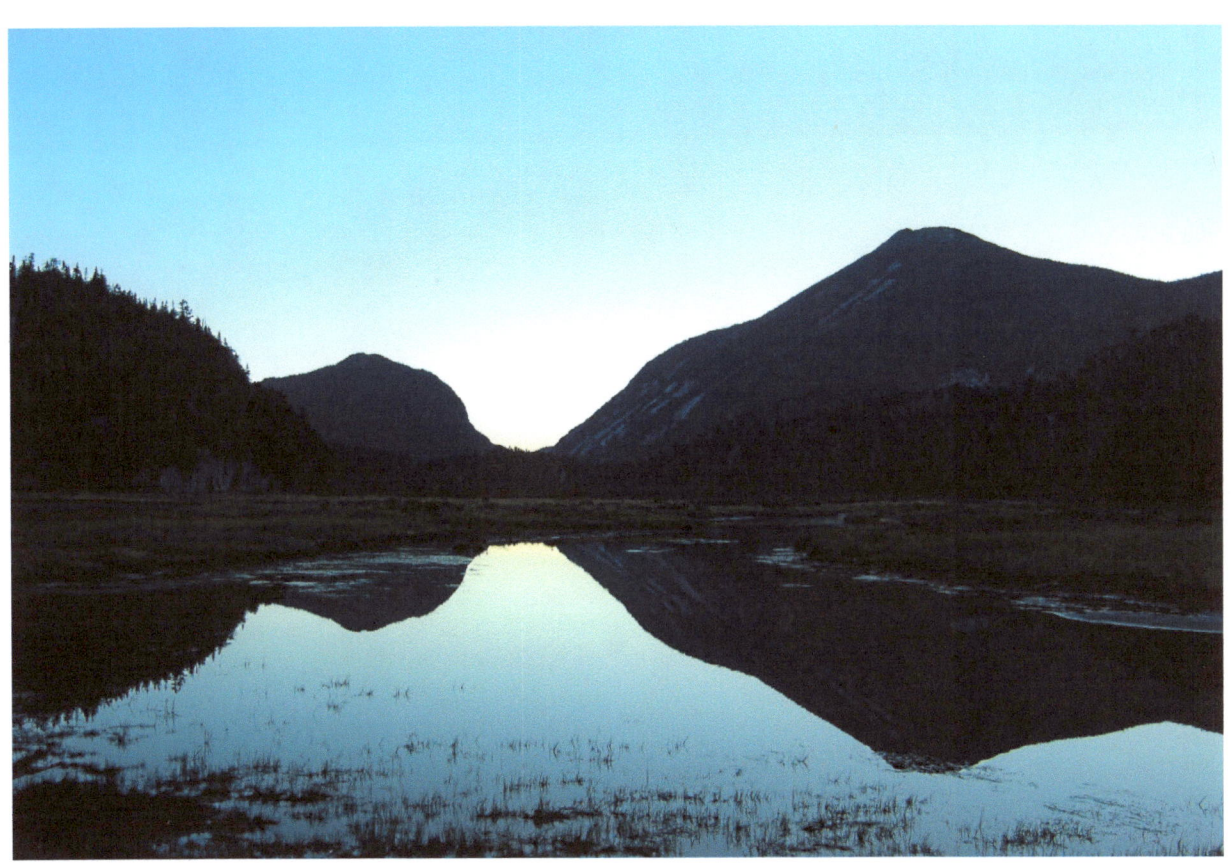

Peaks in the Landscape

A Collection of Haiku

By

Düg Fresh

© ~~02018~~ 2018 Fresh Ink
Skahnéhtati, New York

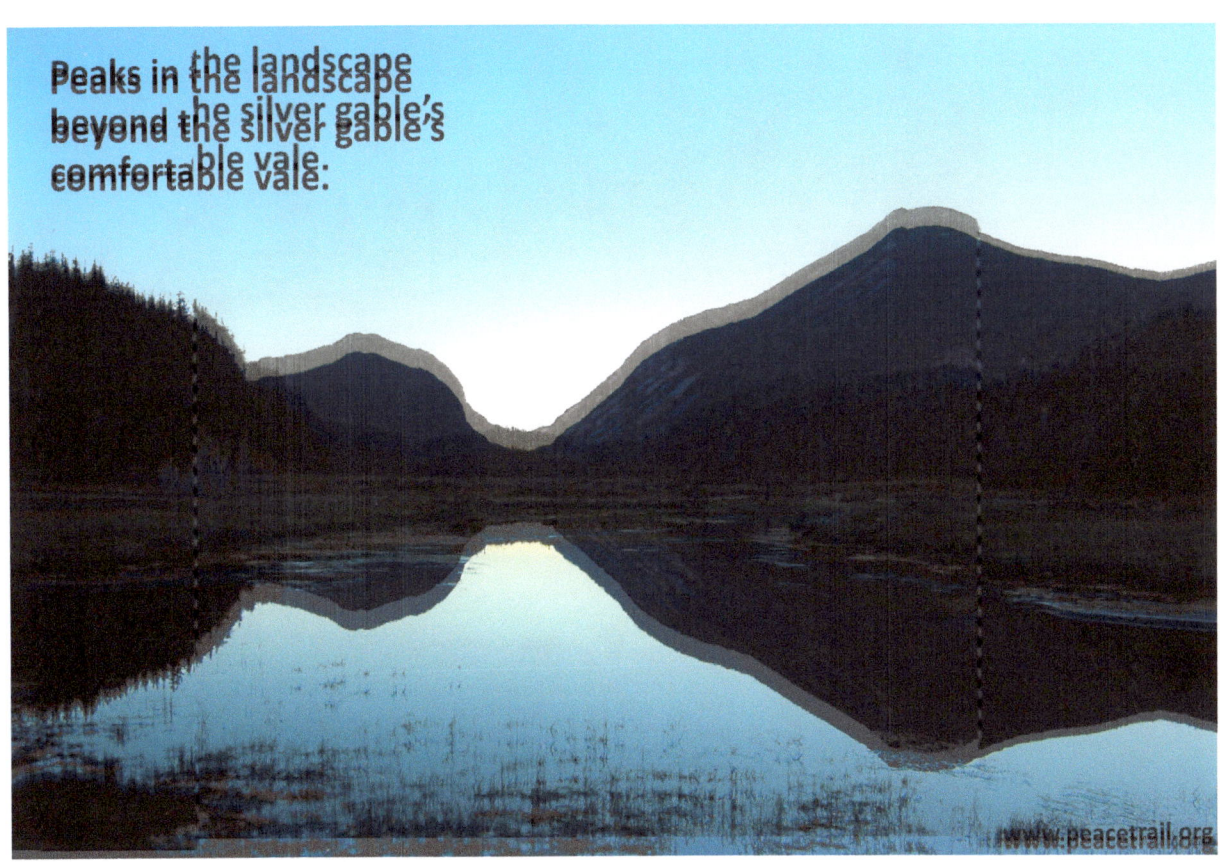

Peaks in the landscape
beyond the silver gable's
comfortable vale:

www.peacetrail.org

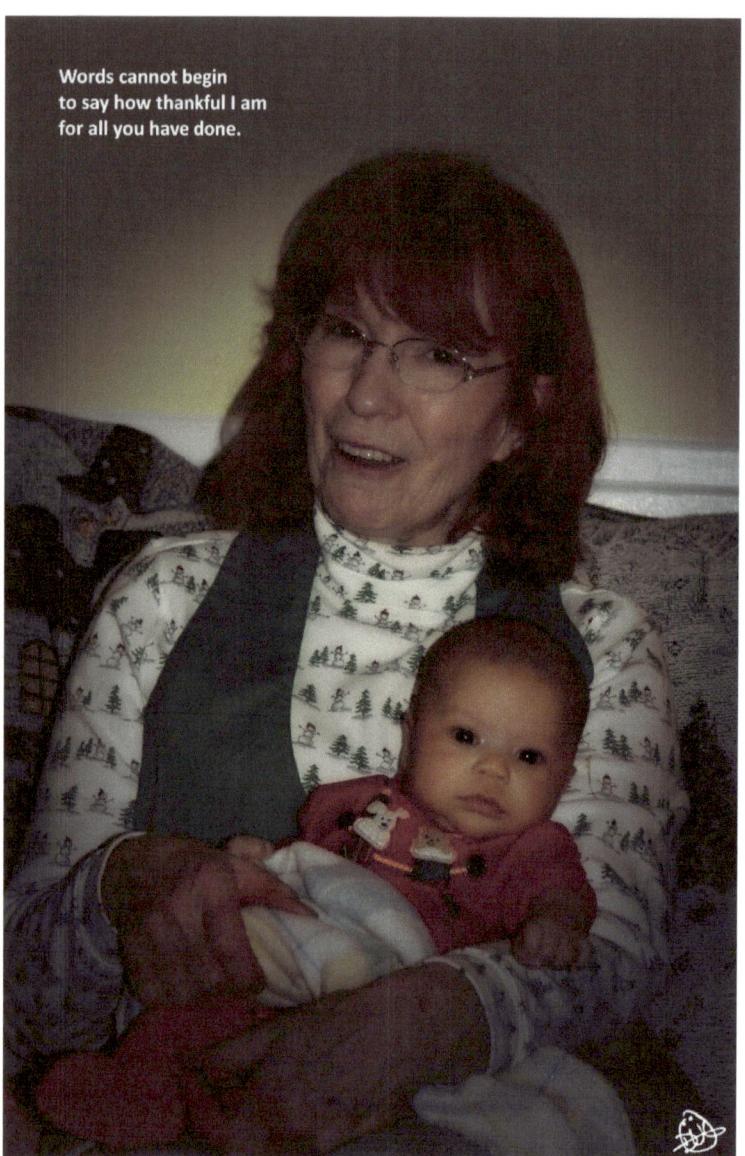

Dedication:

To my mom because no matter what, she still loves me.
There is no small miracle in that.

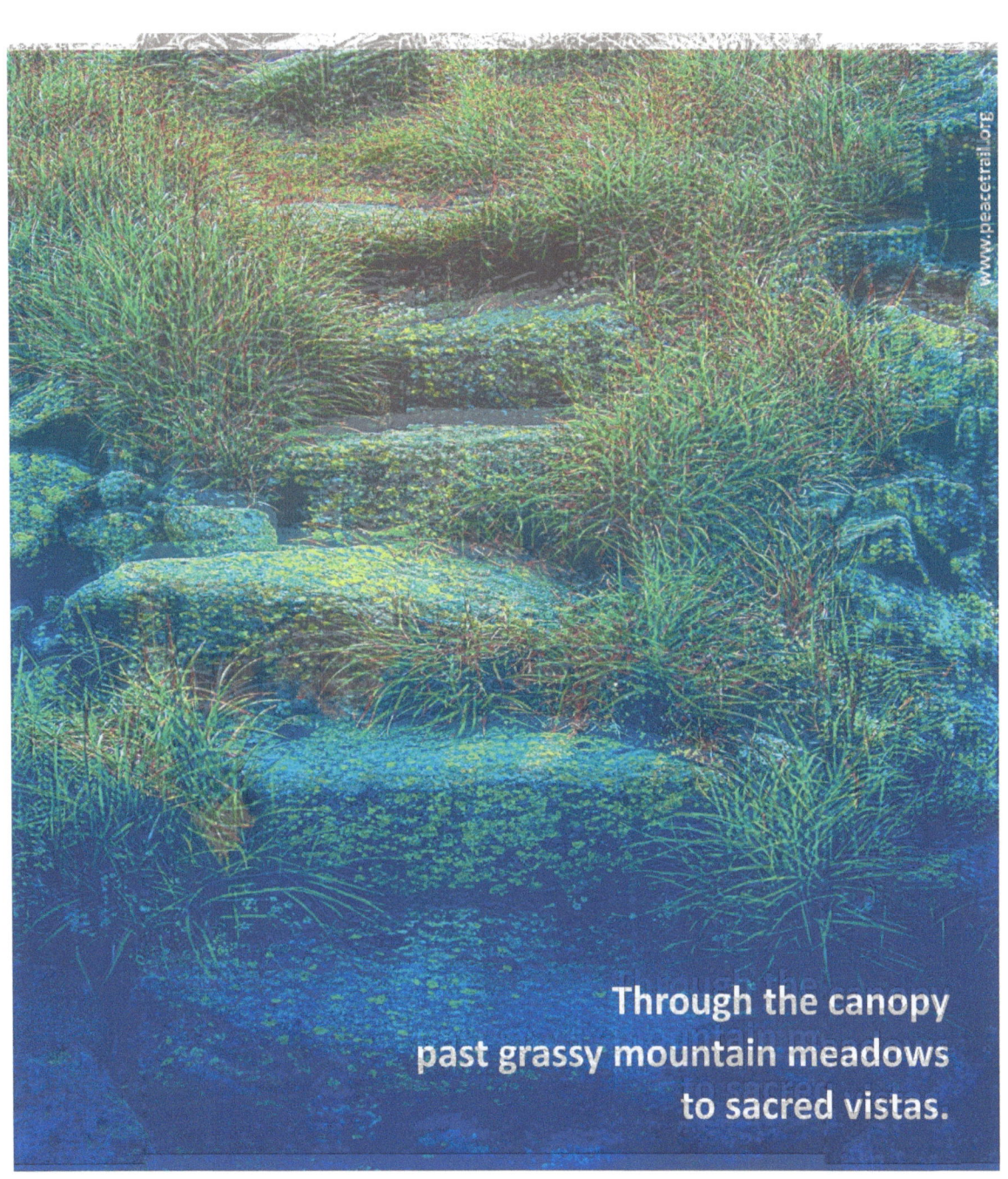

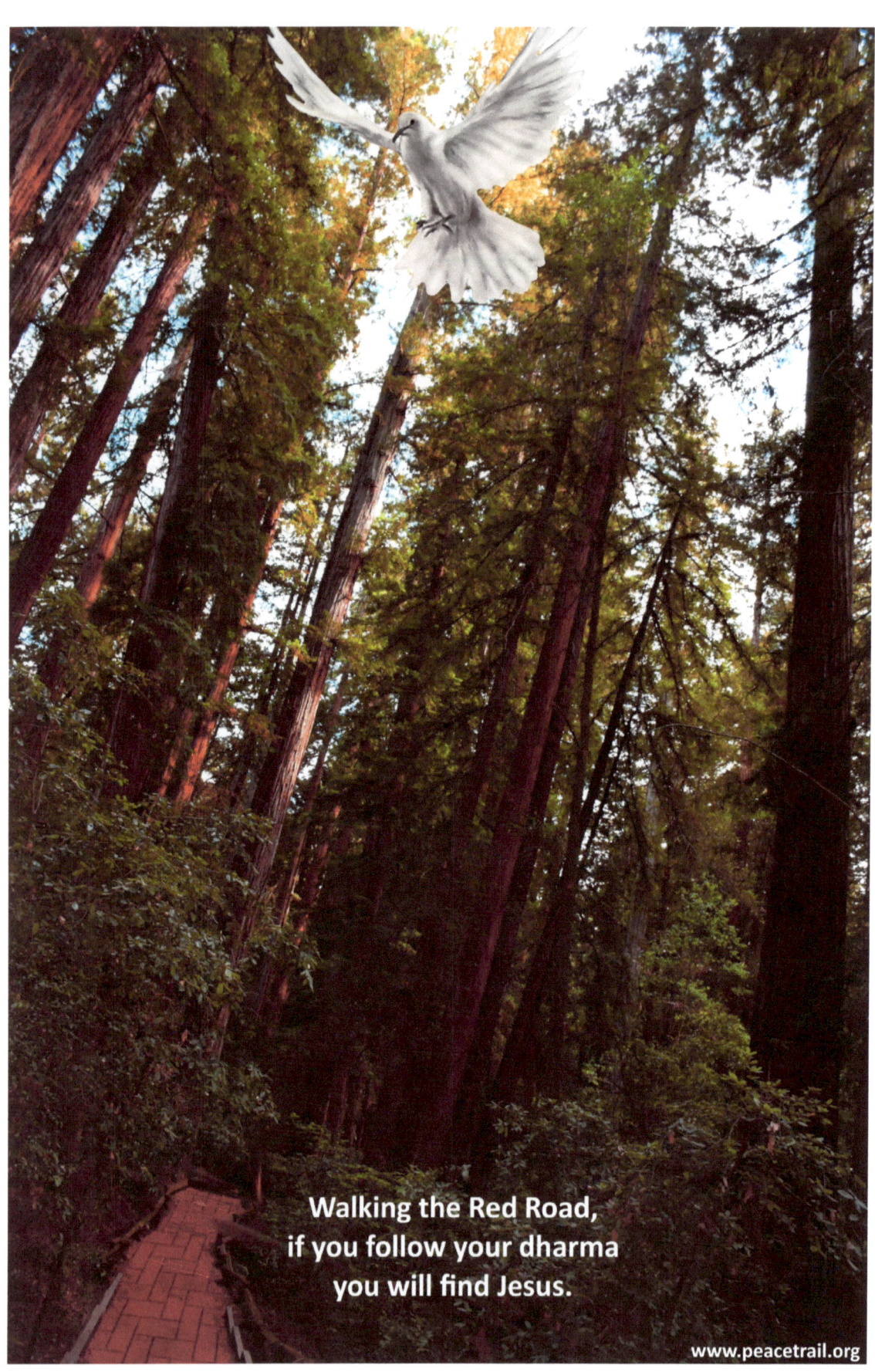

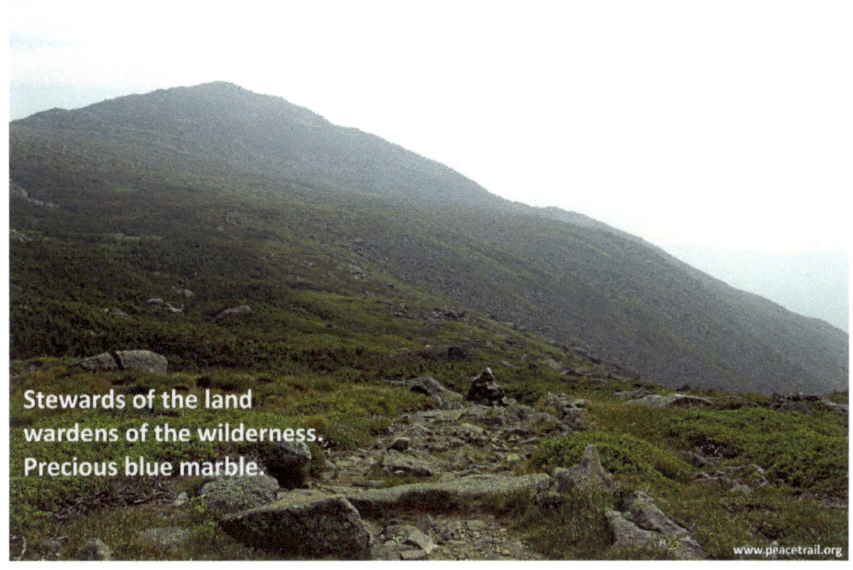

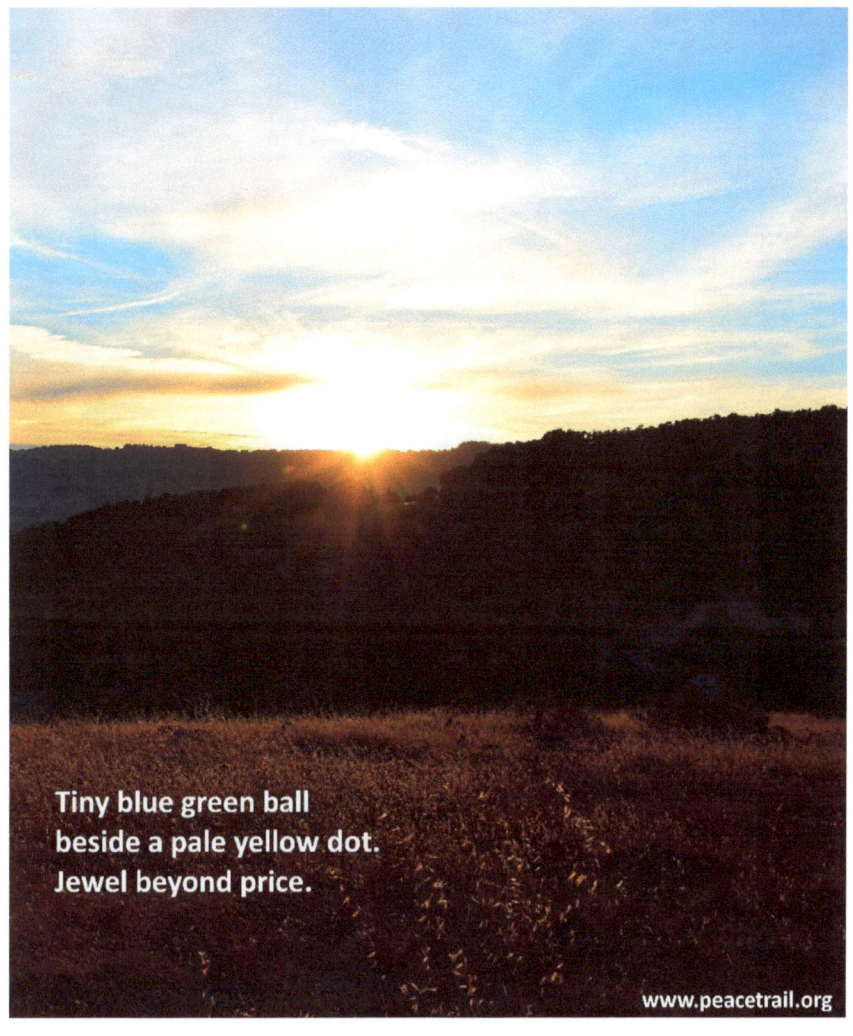

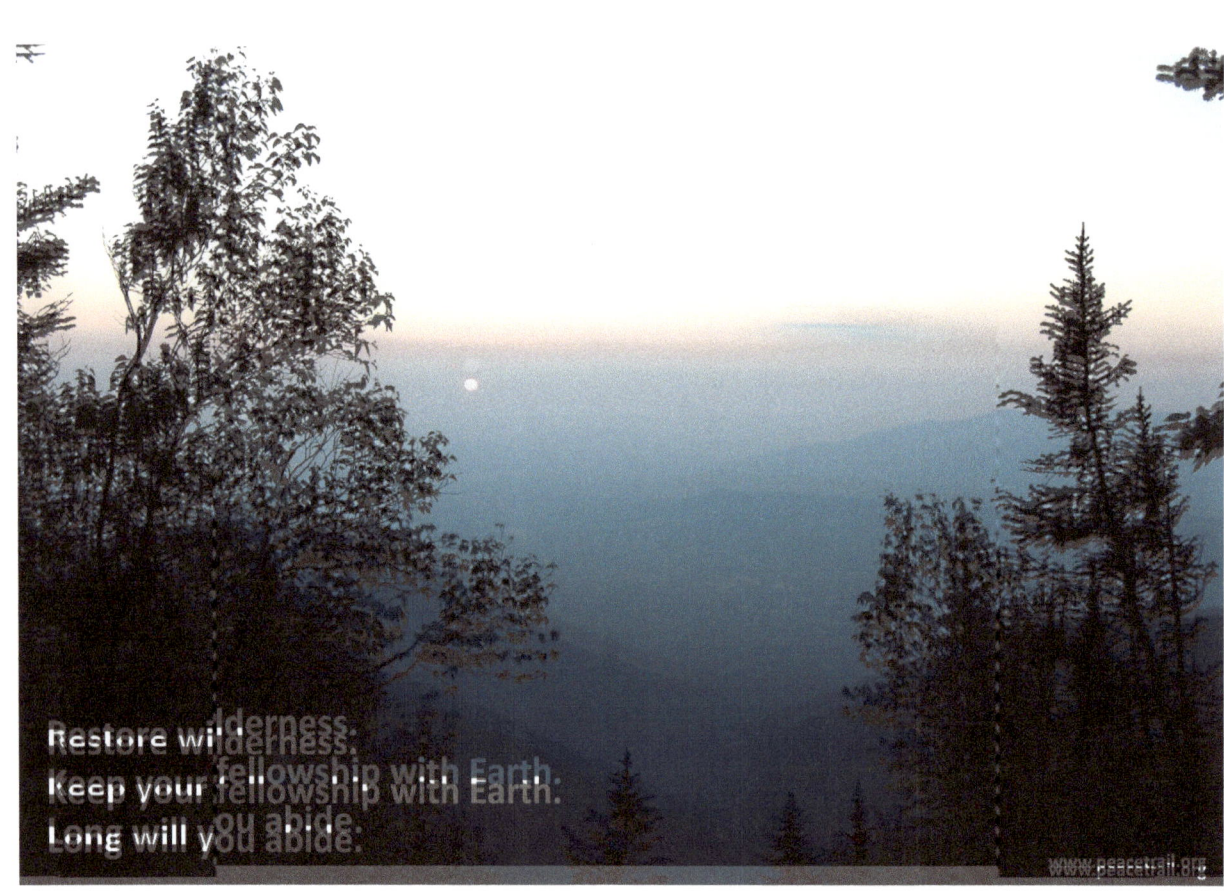

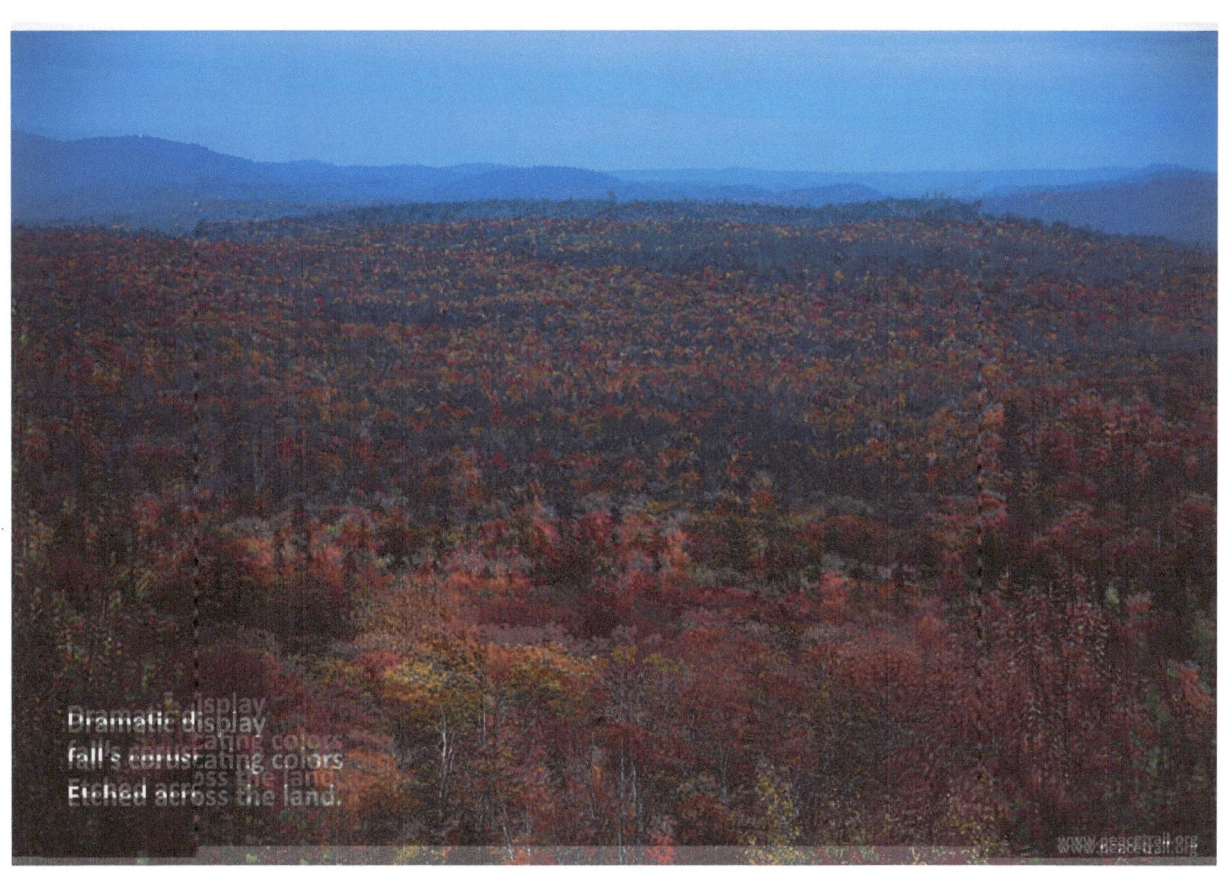

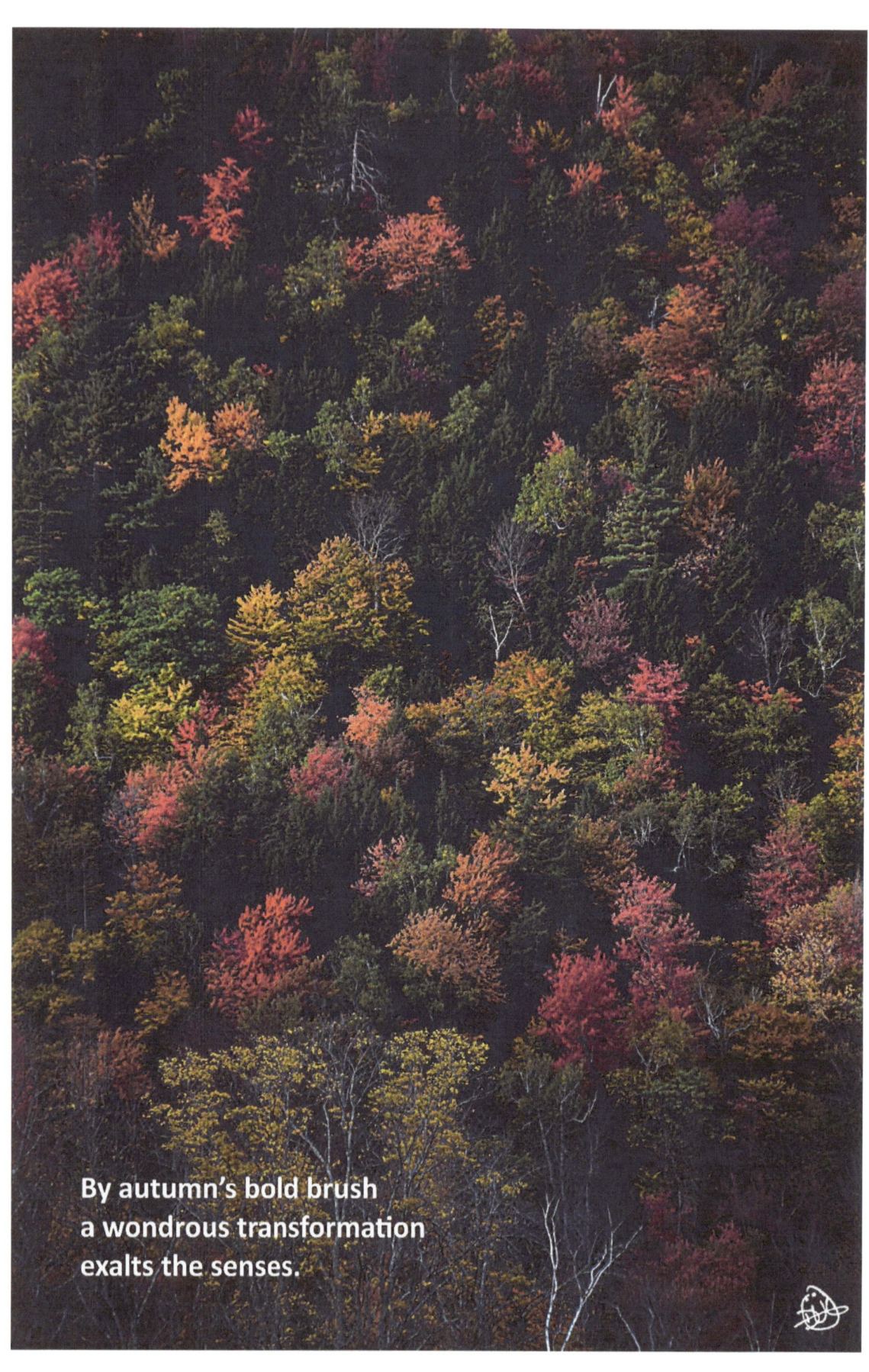

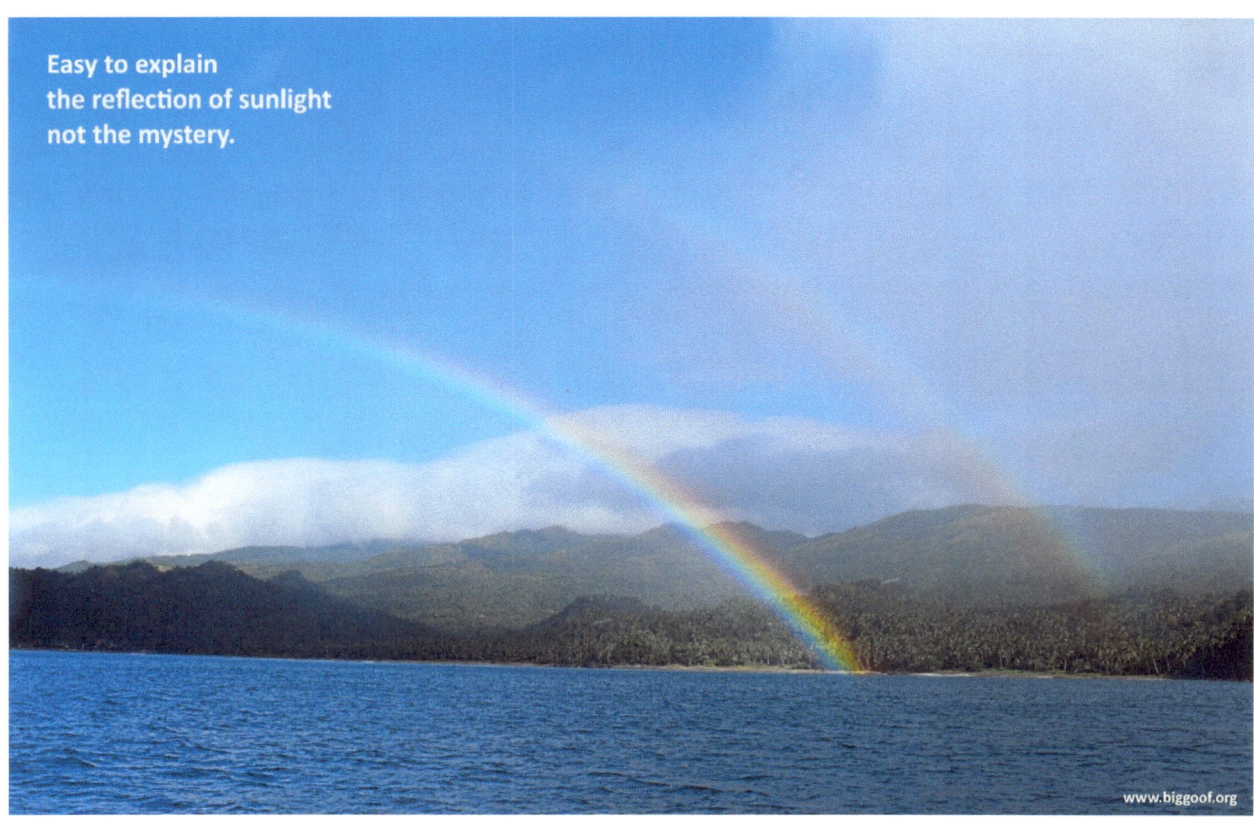

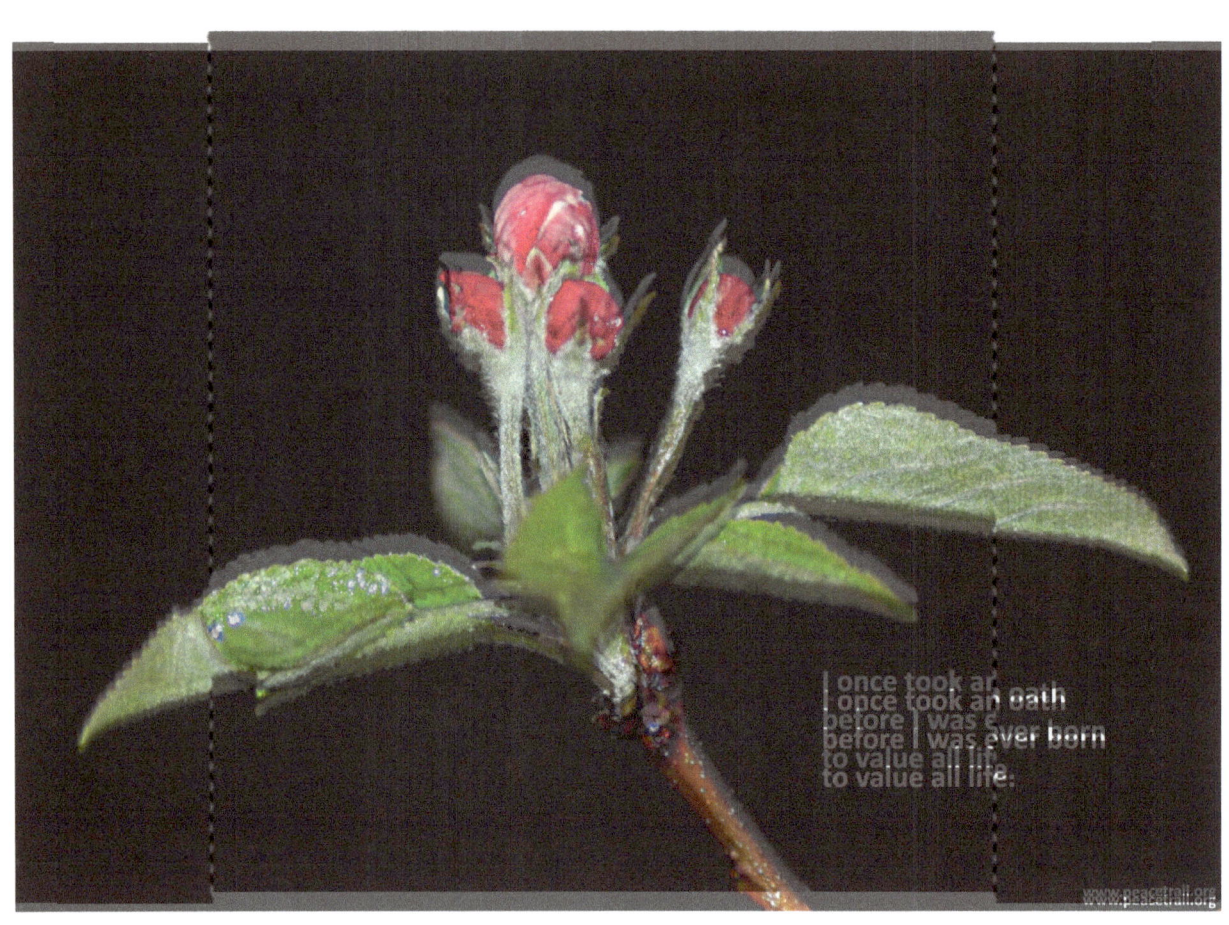

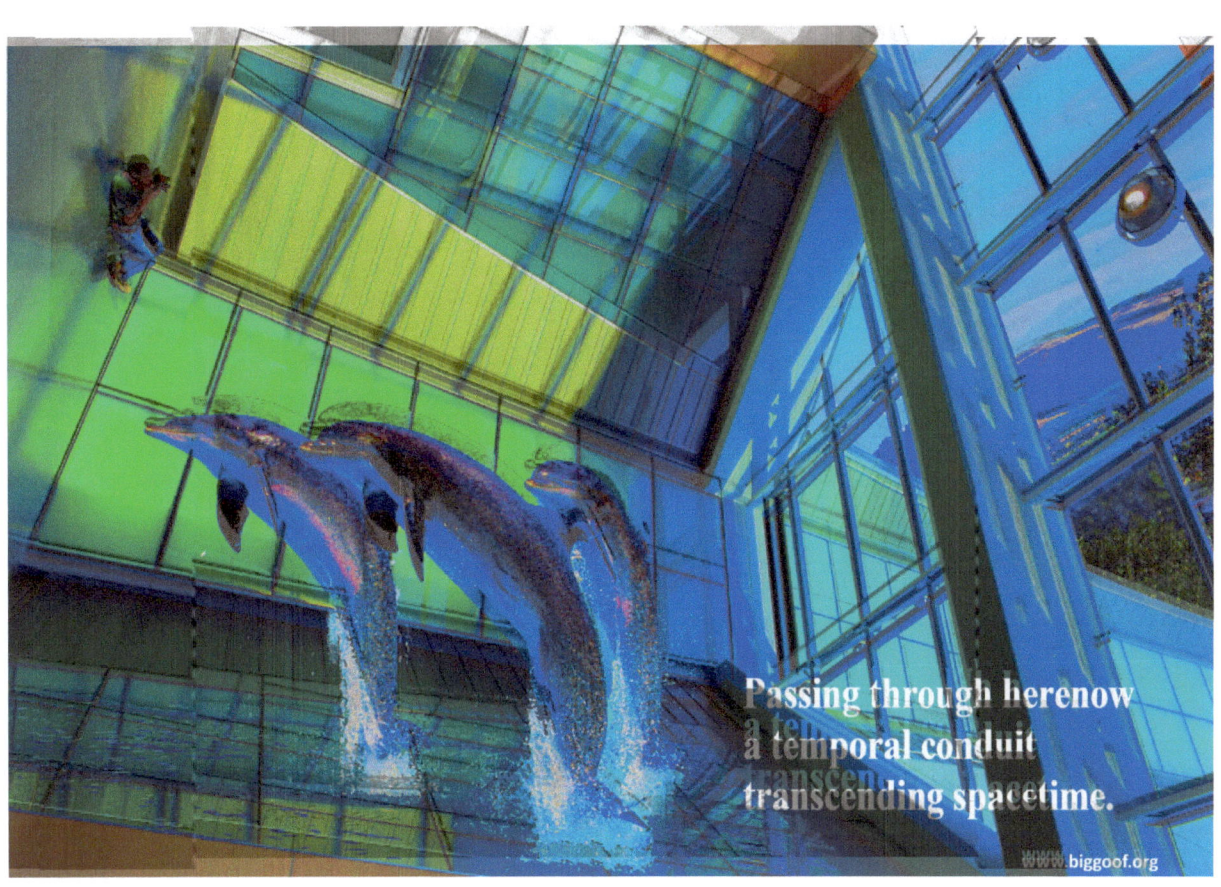

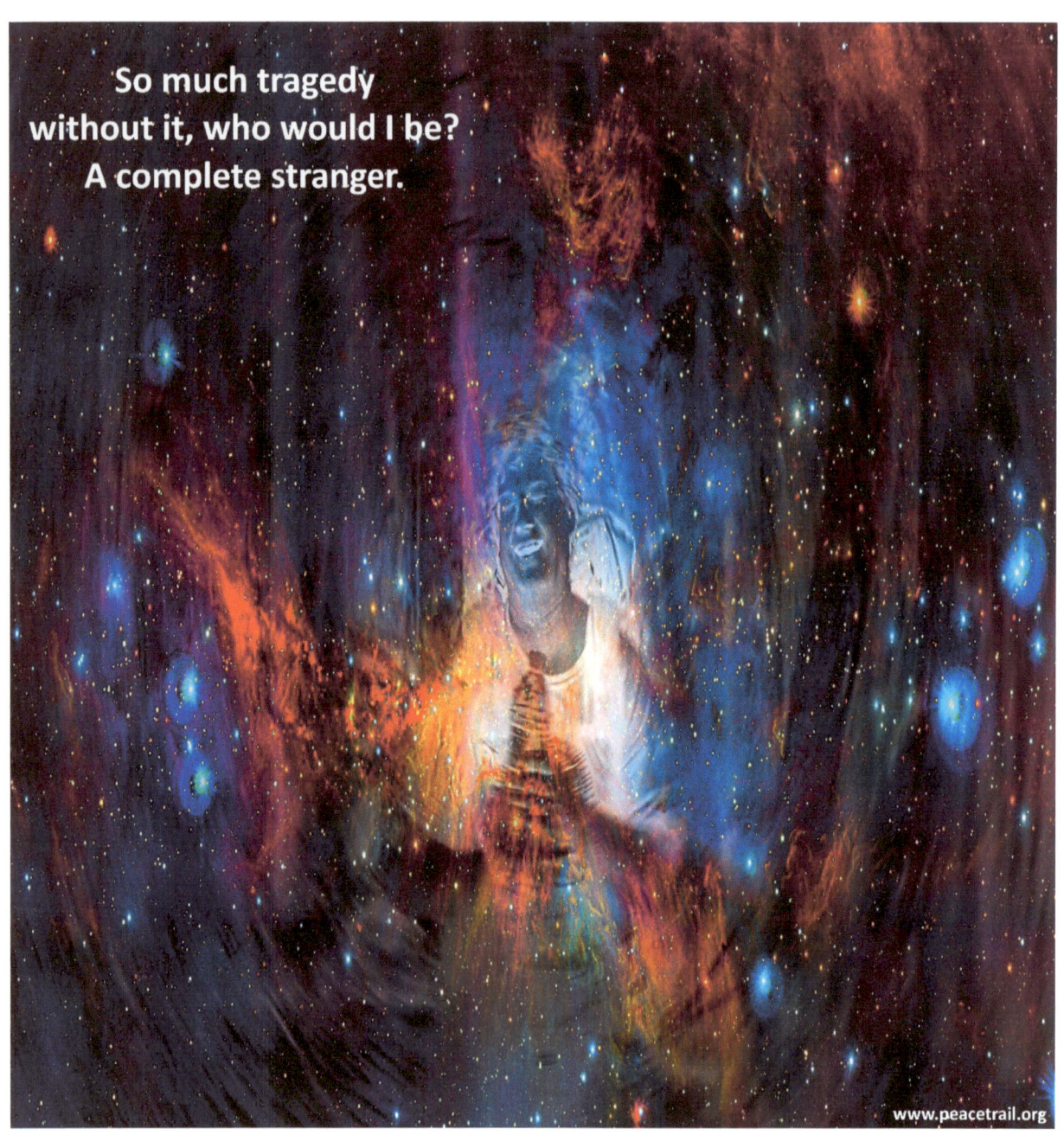

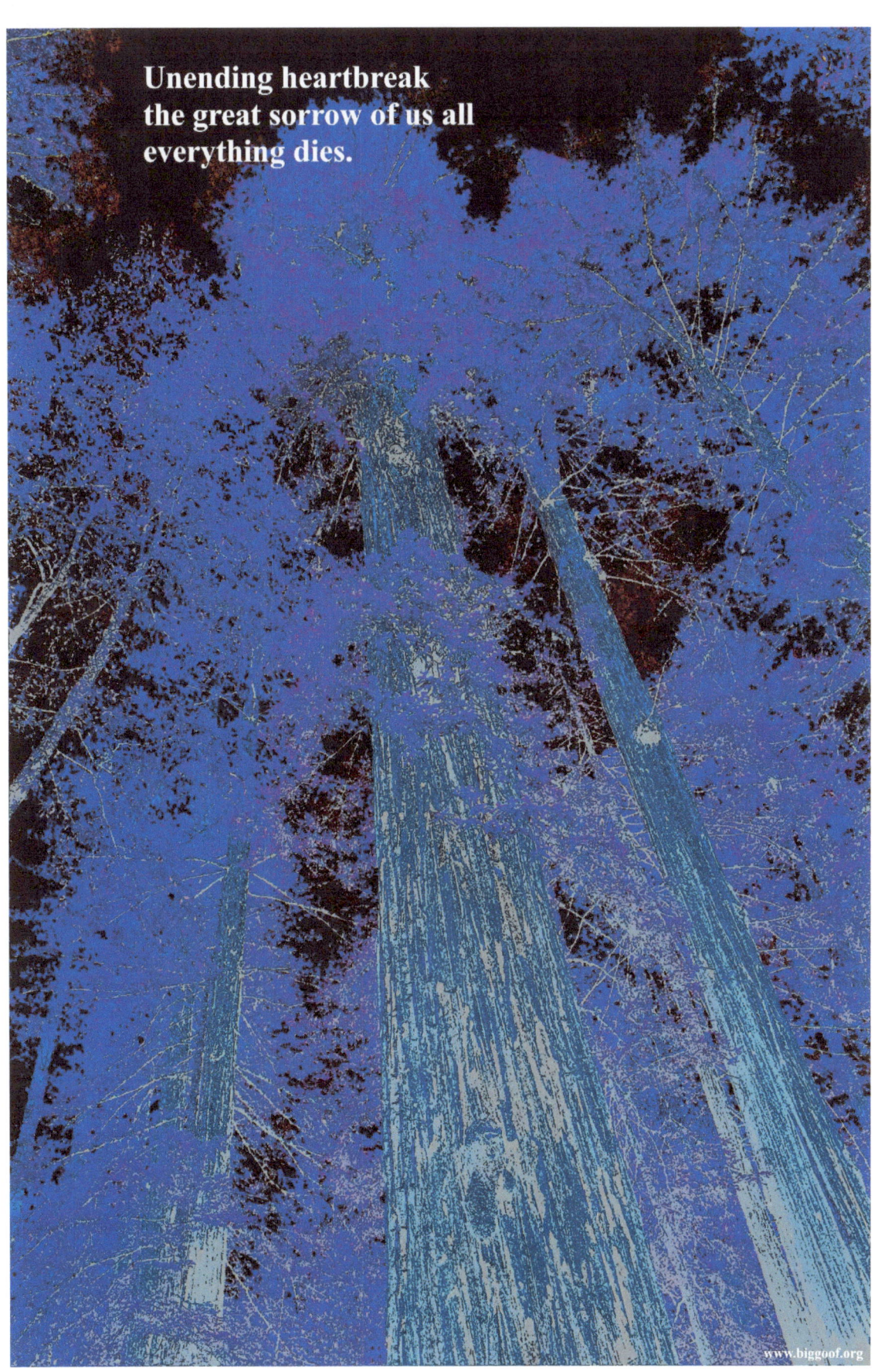

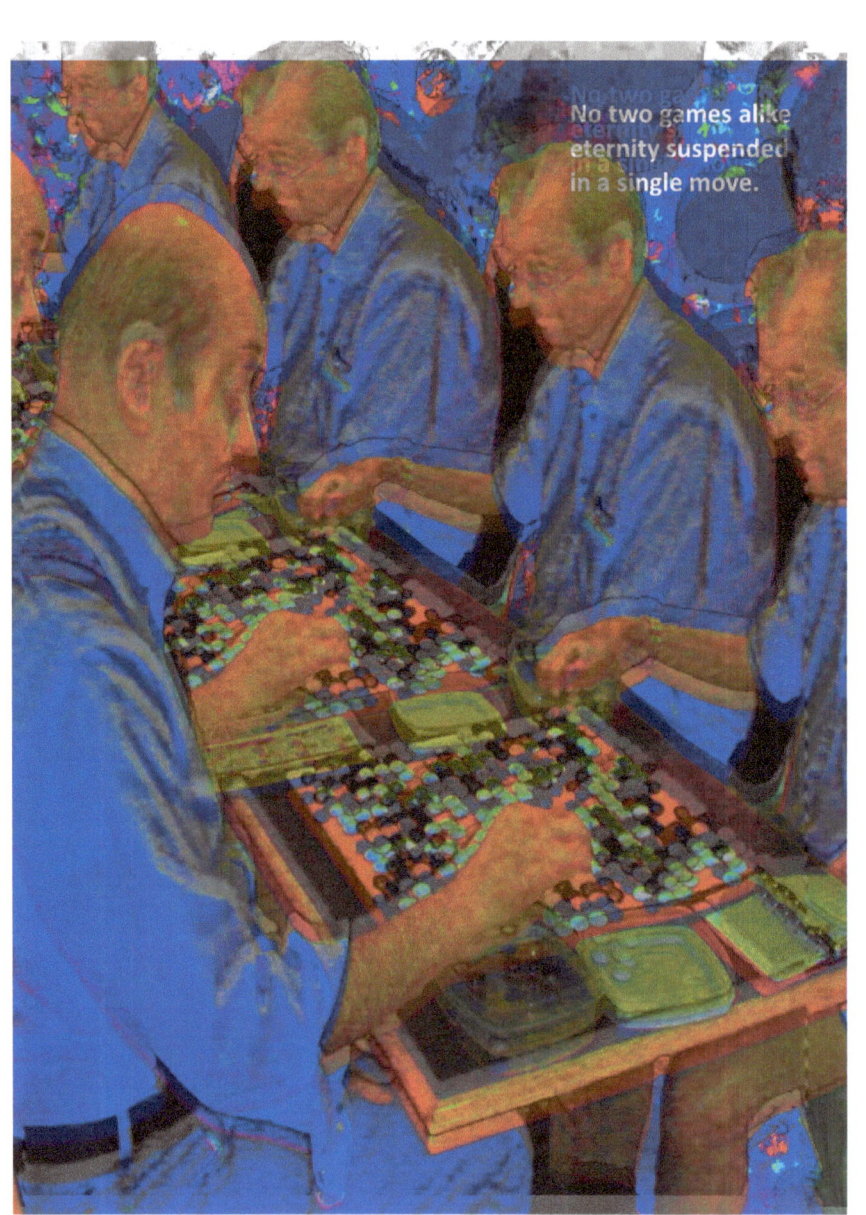

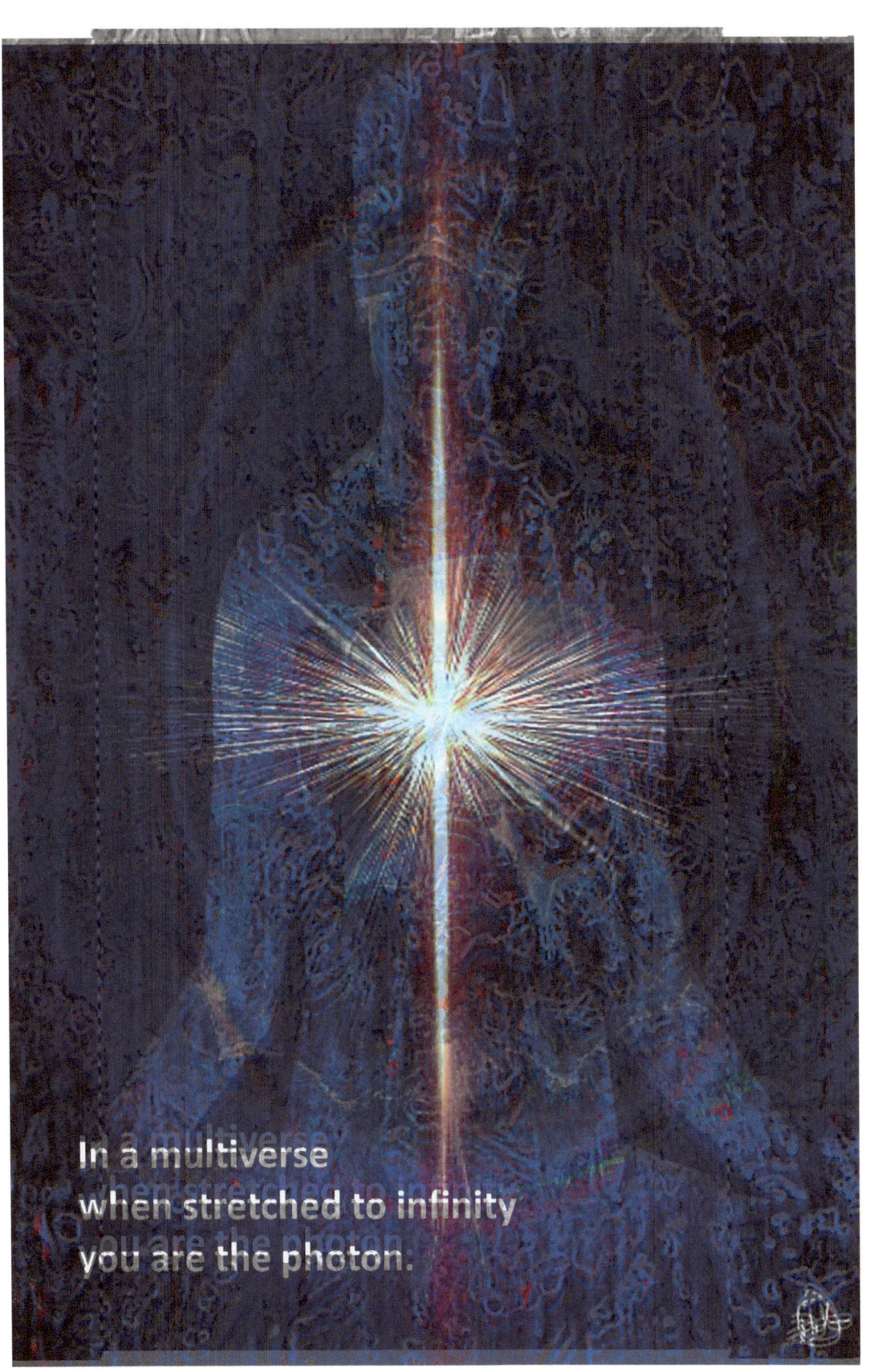

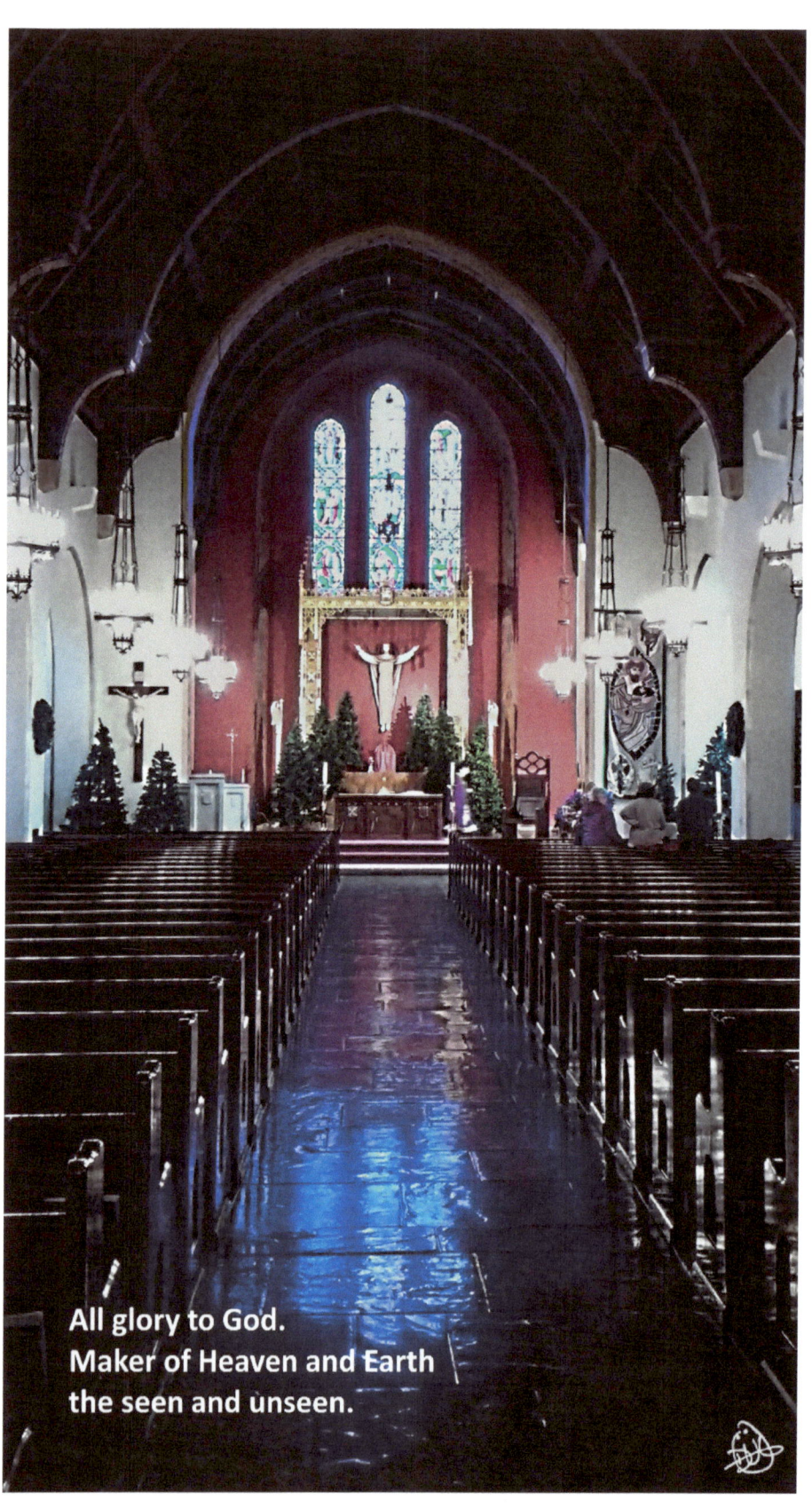

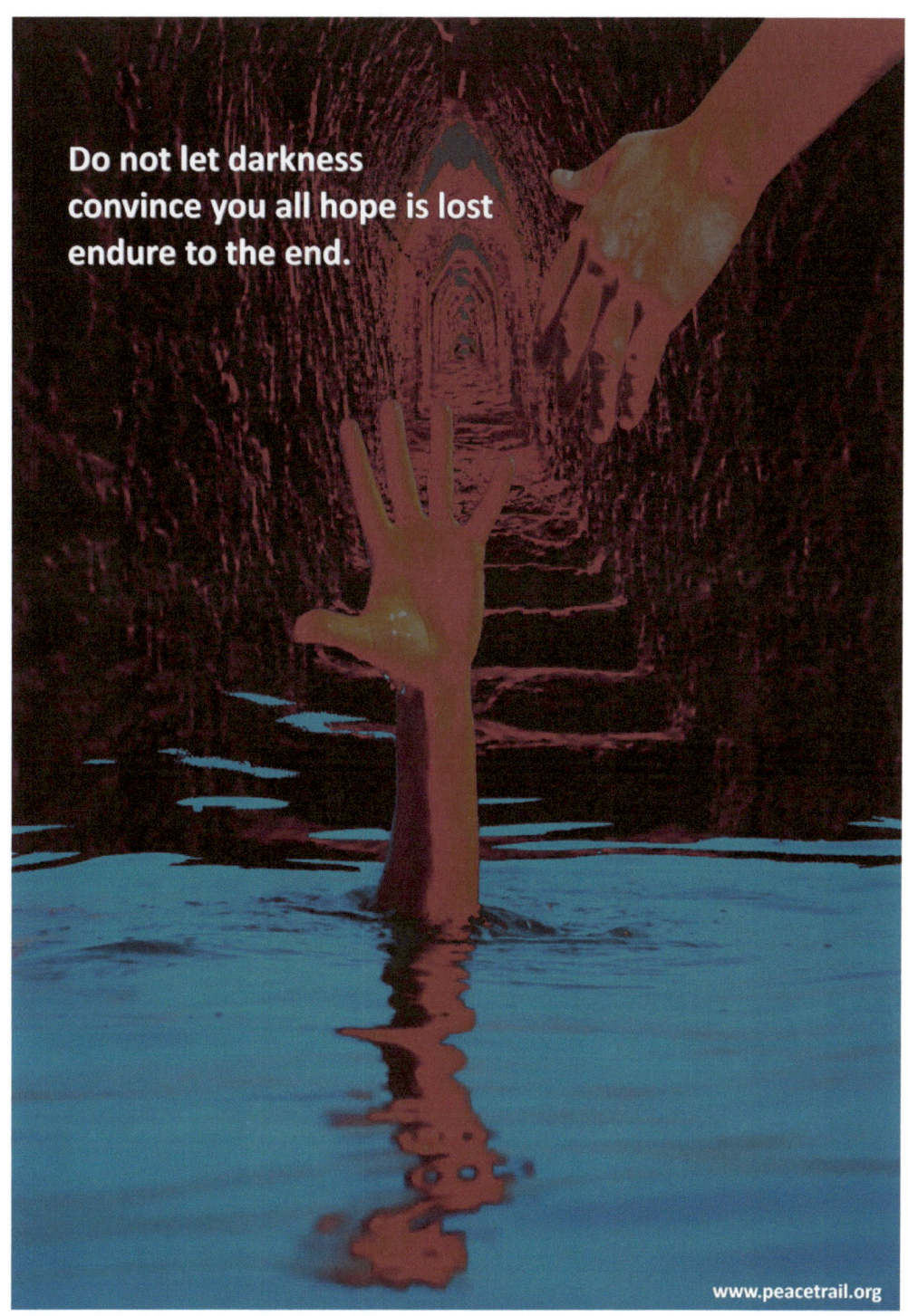

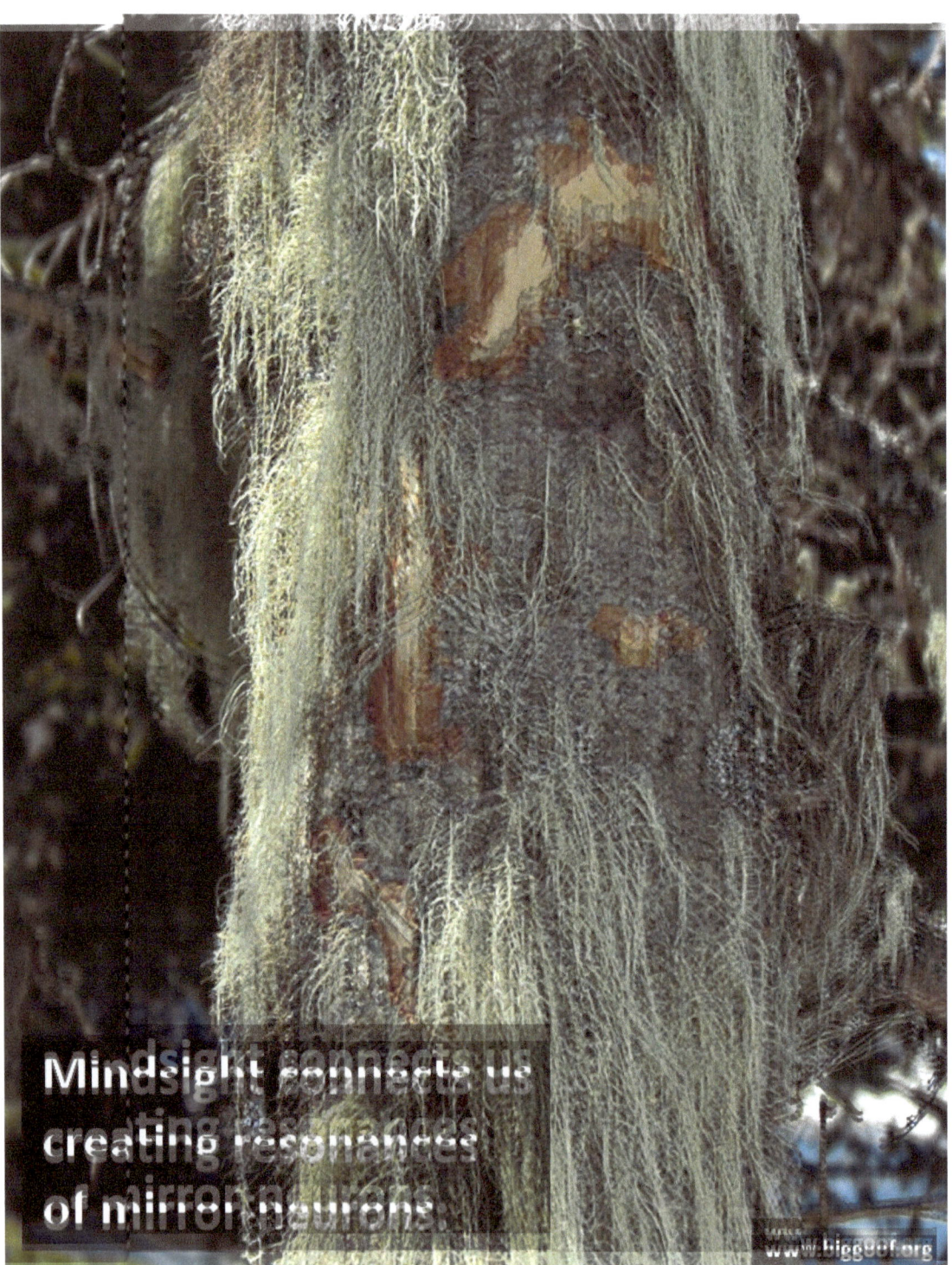

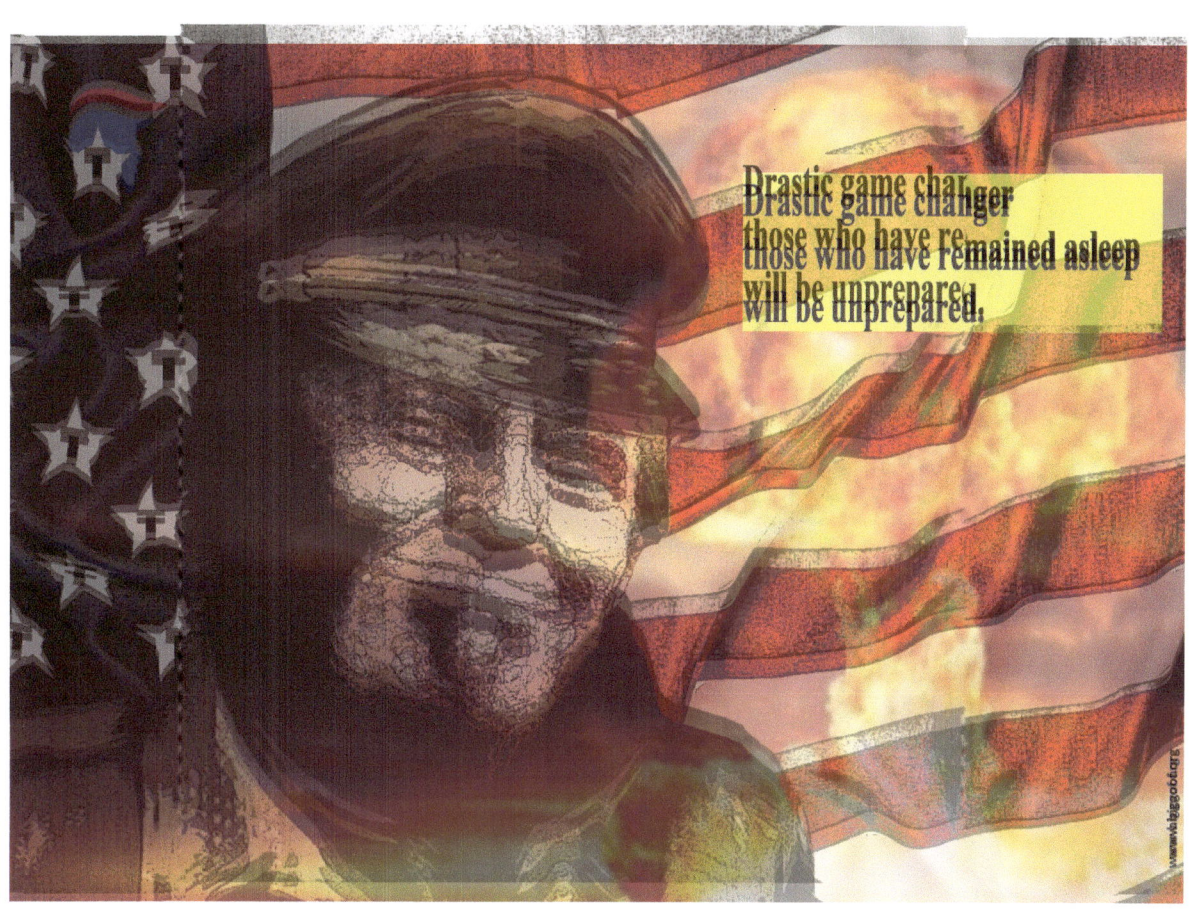

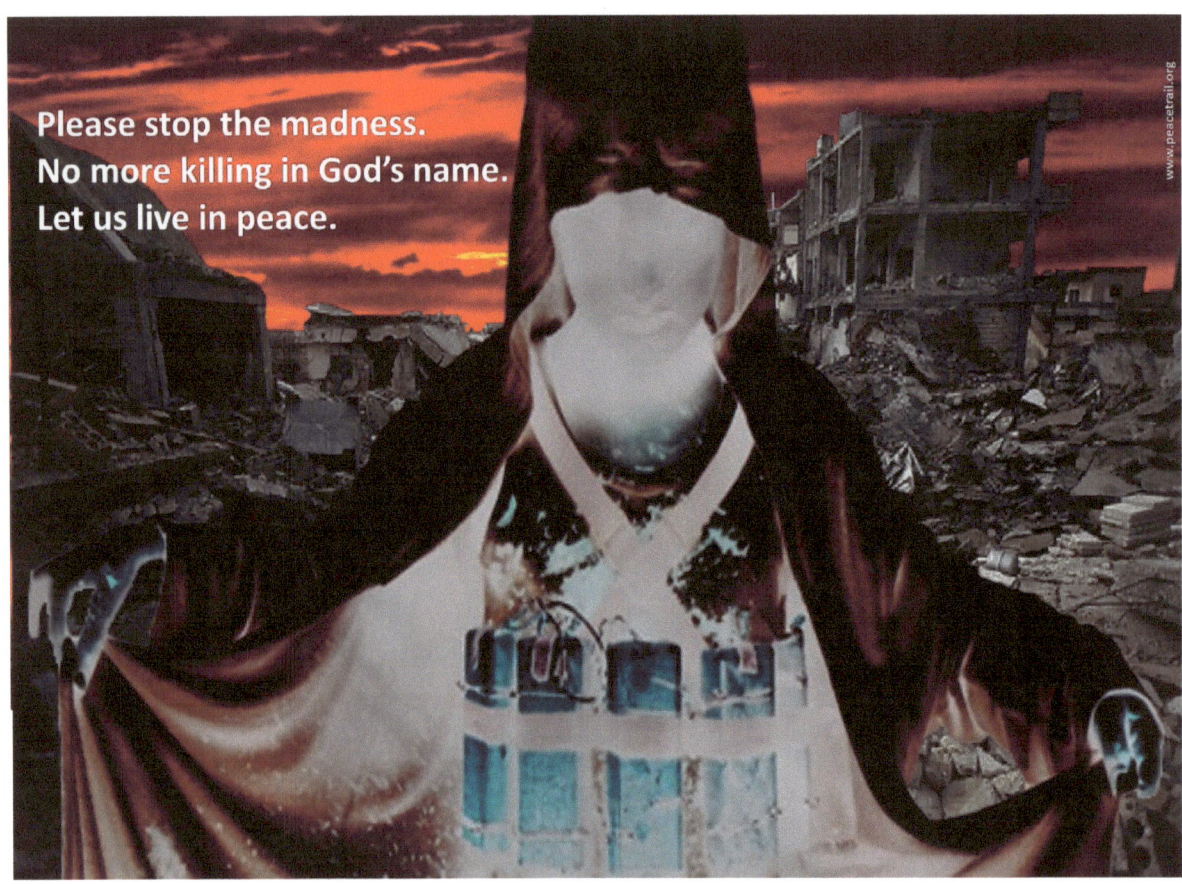

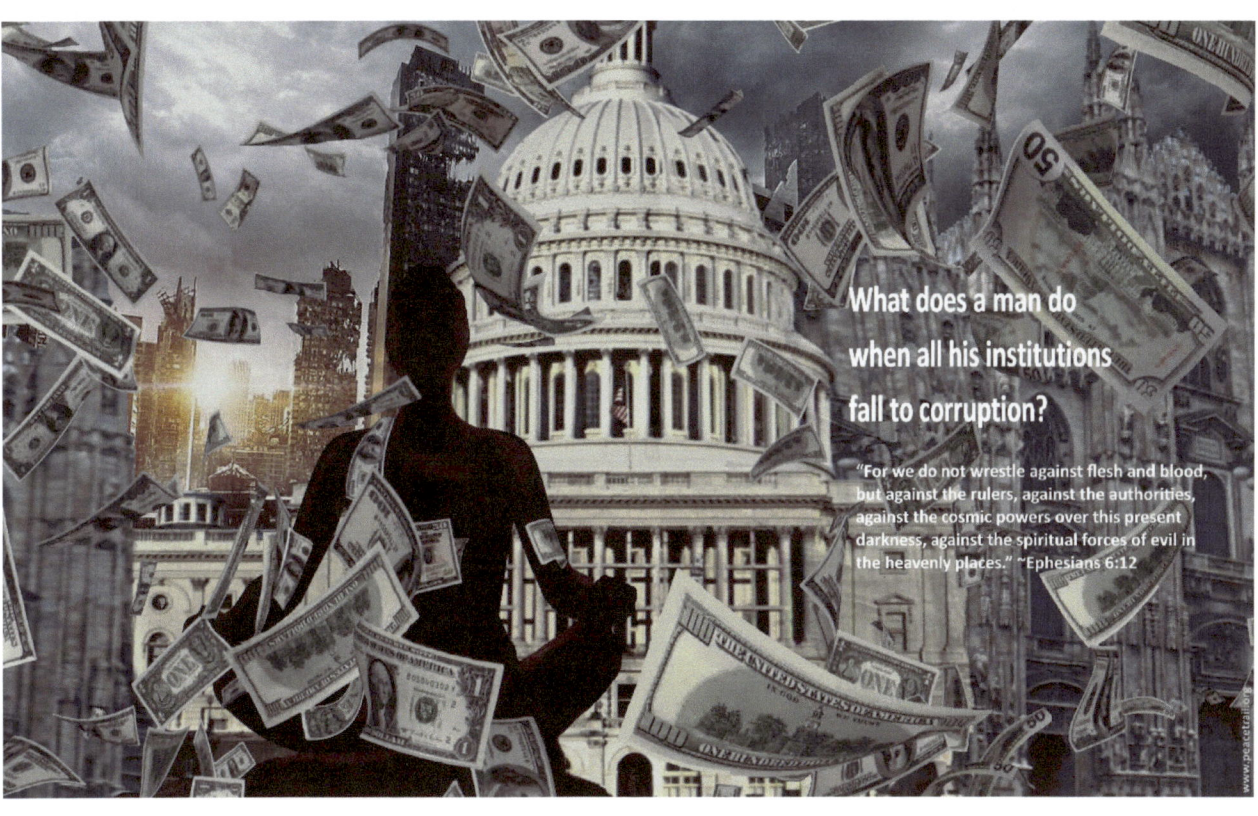

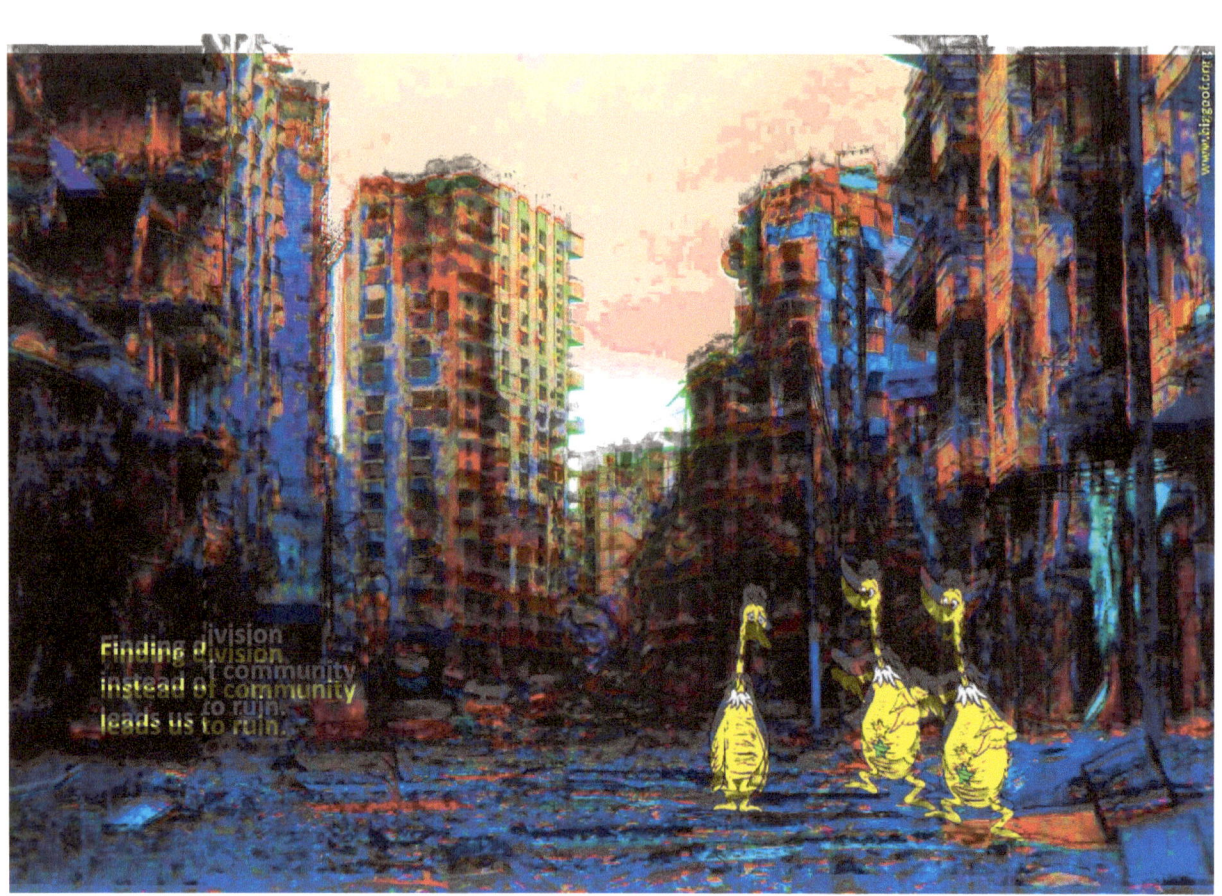

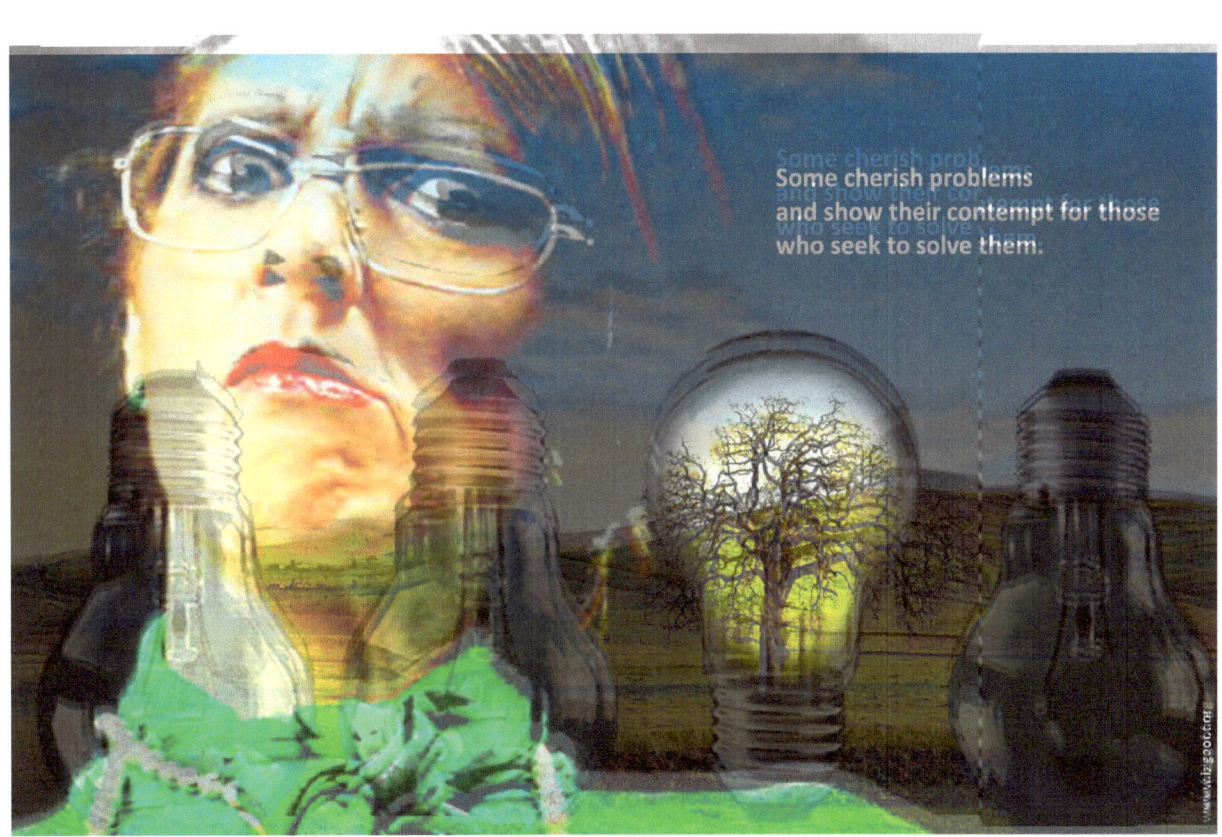

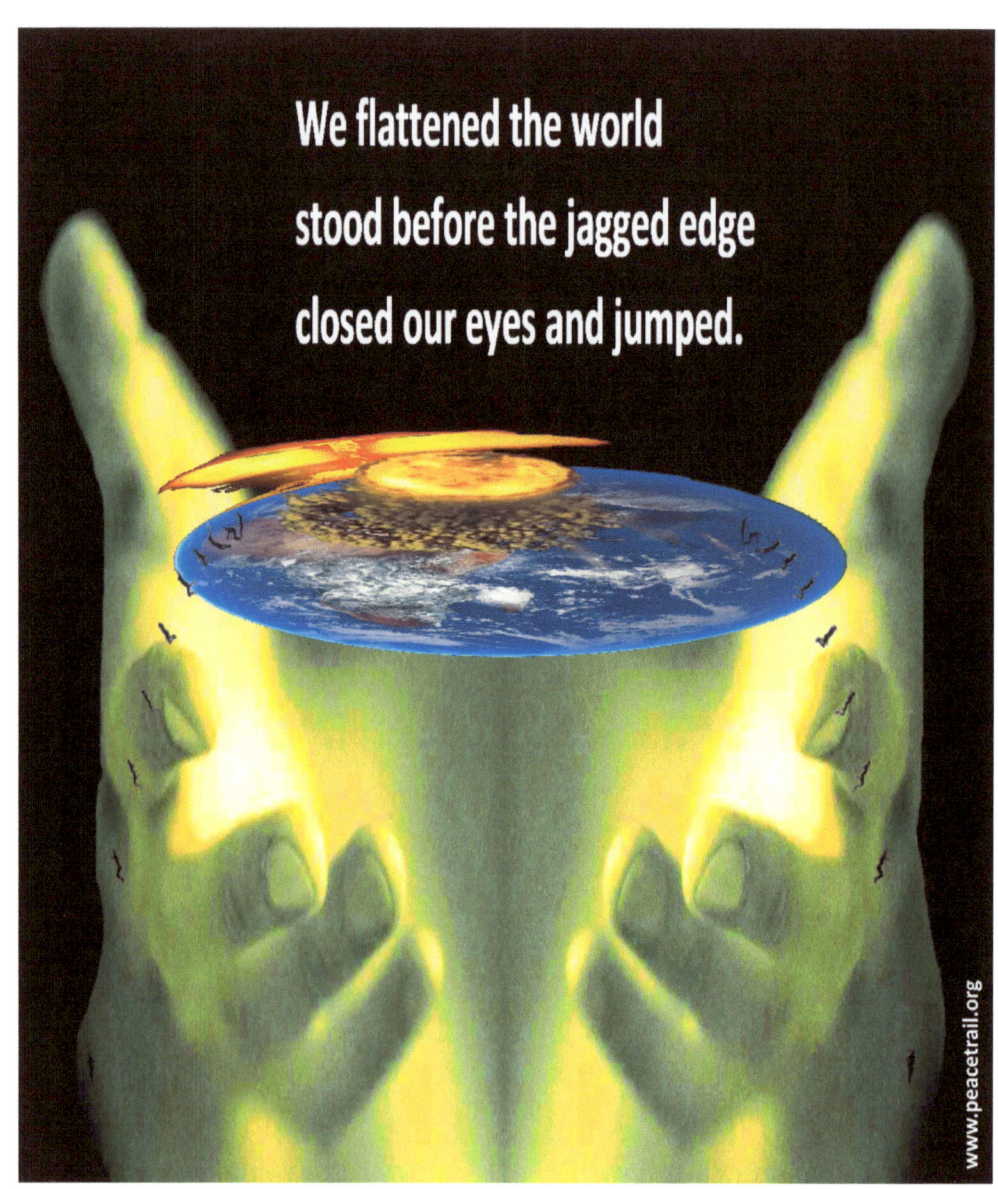

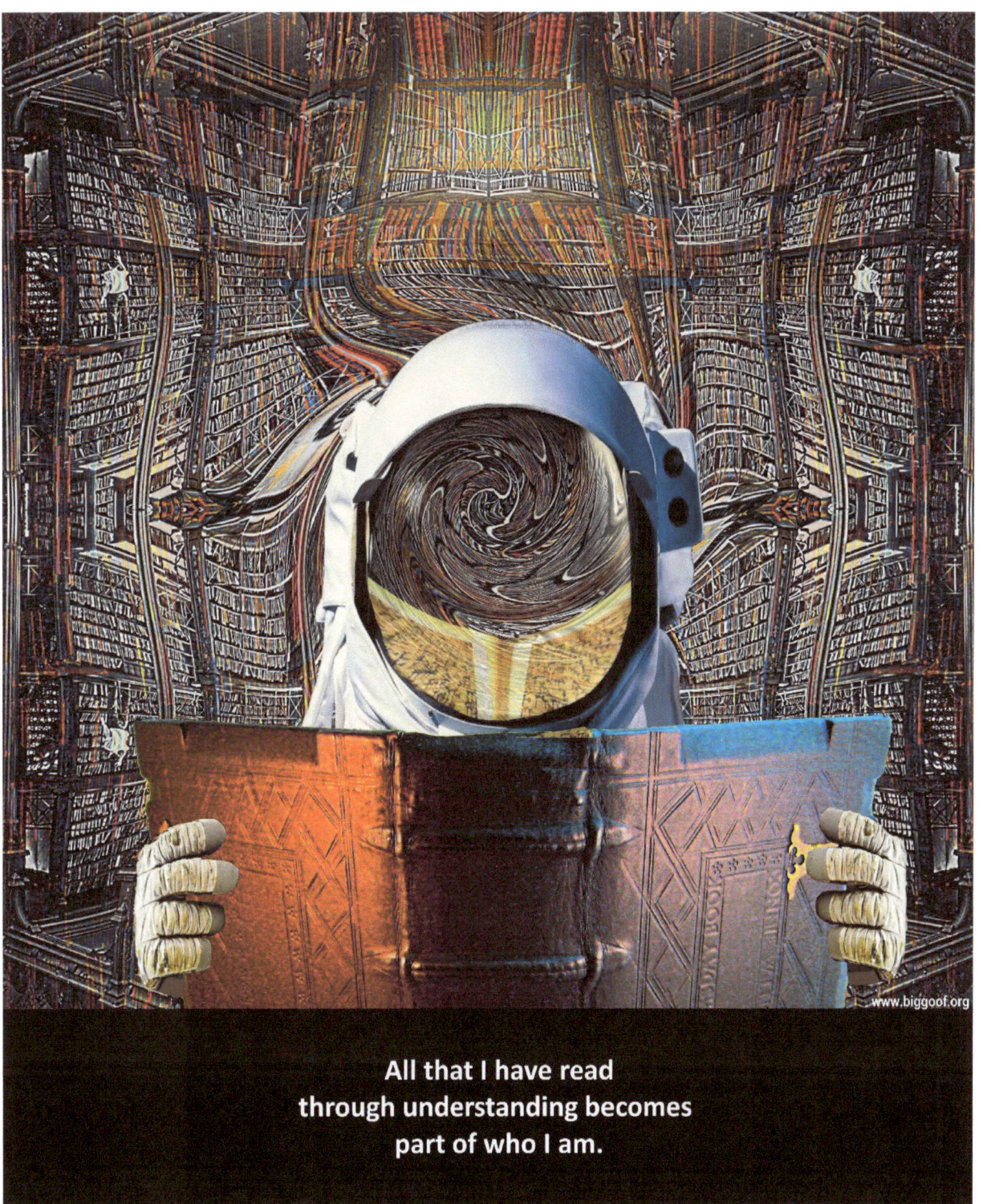

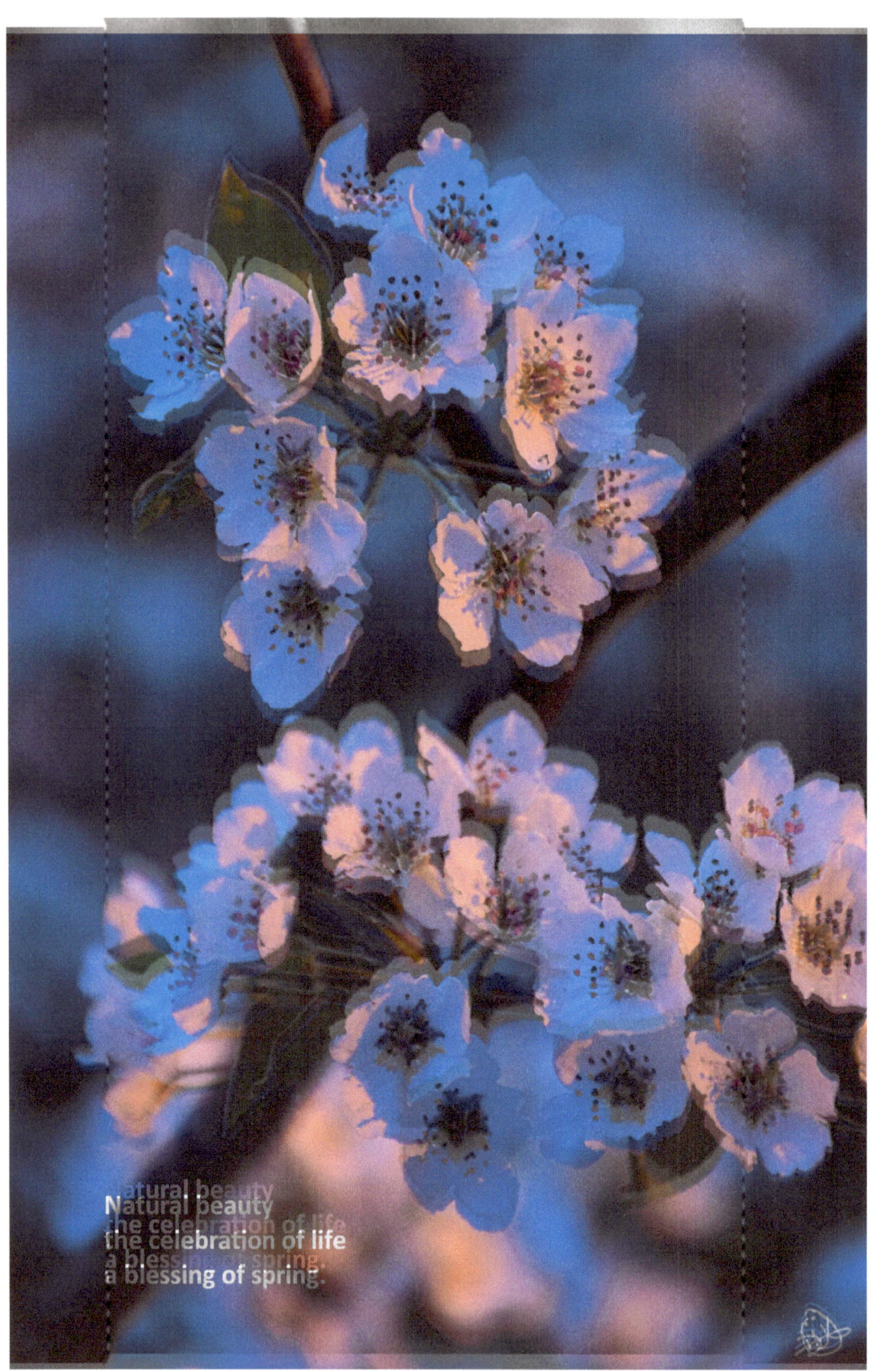

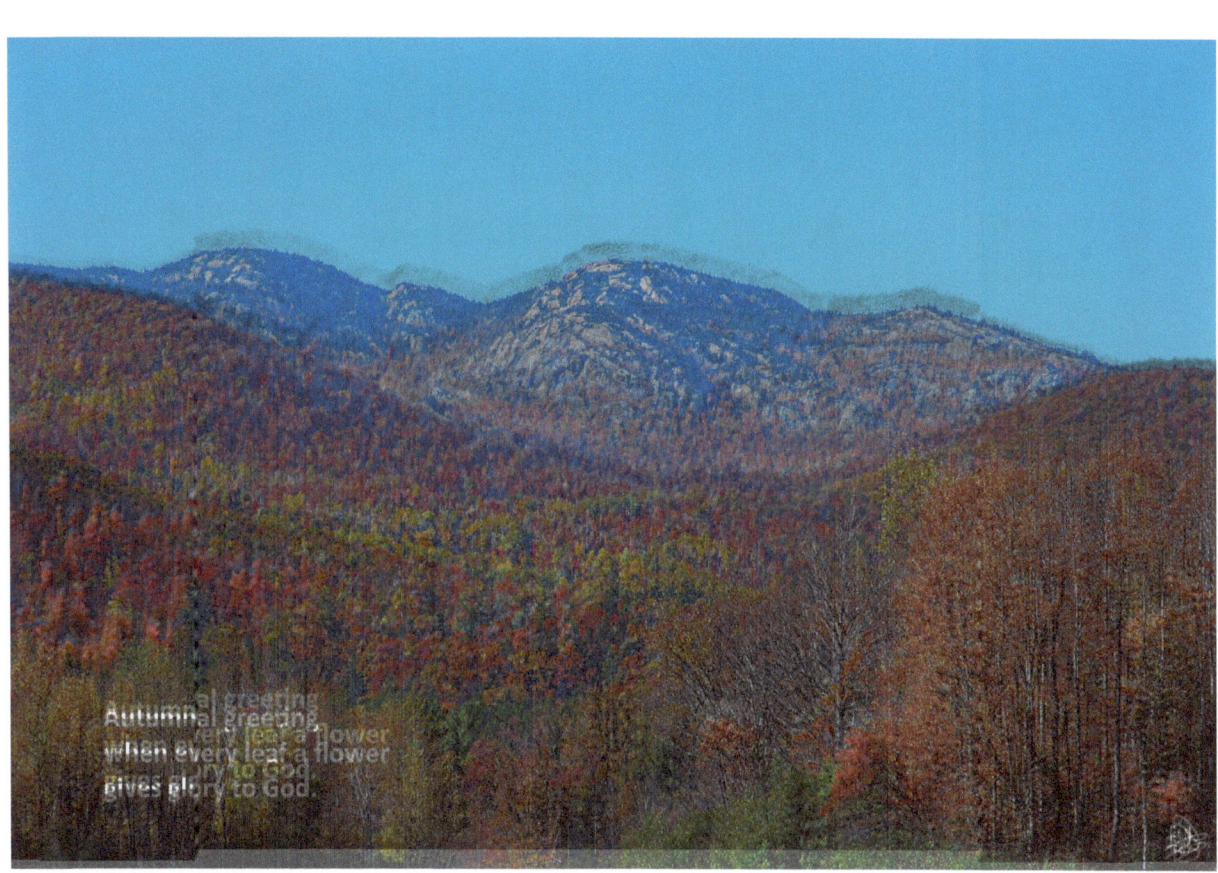

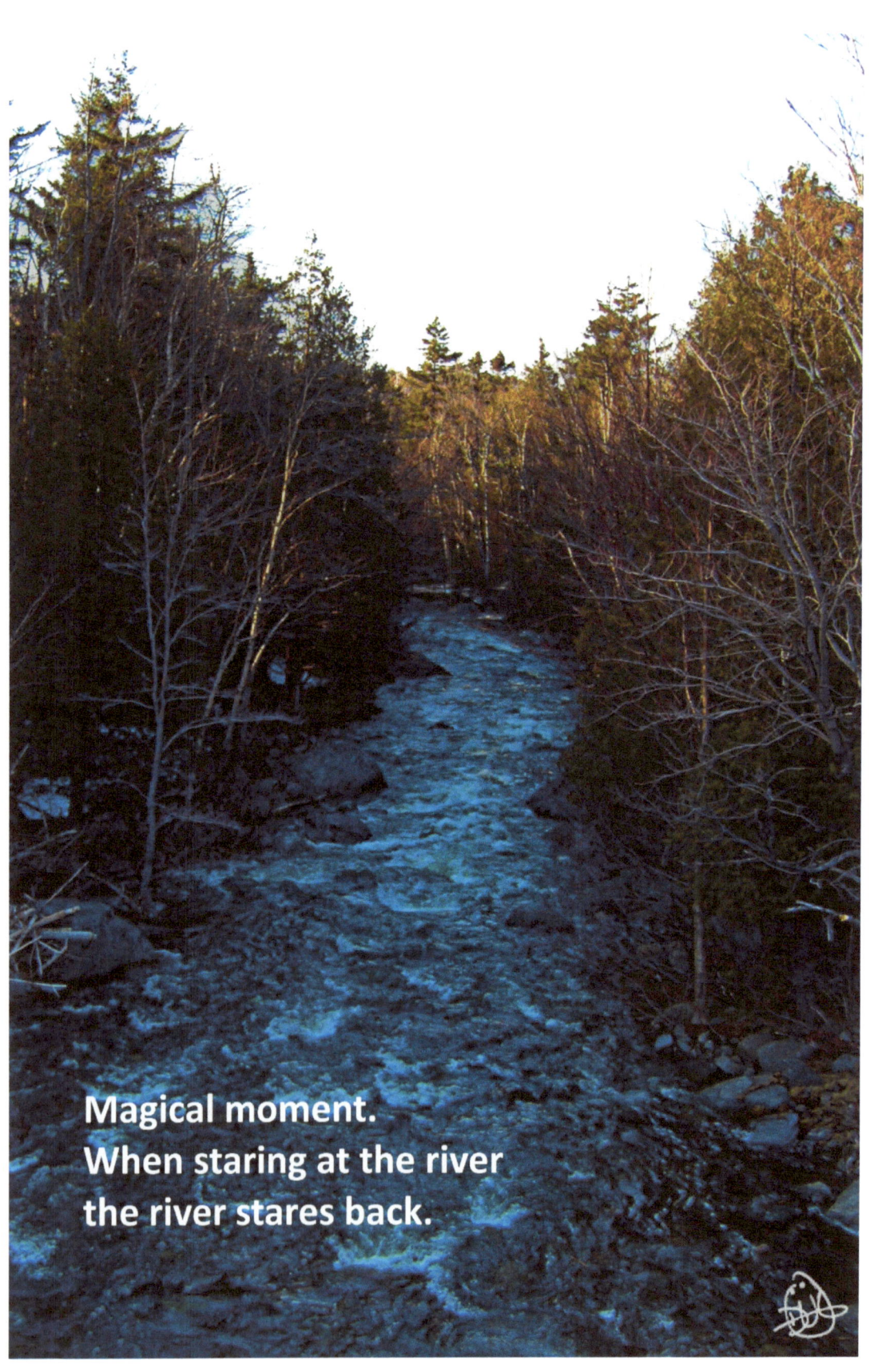

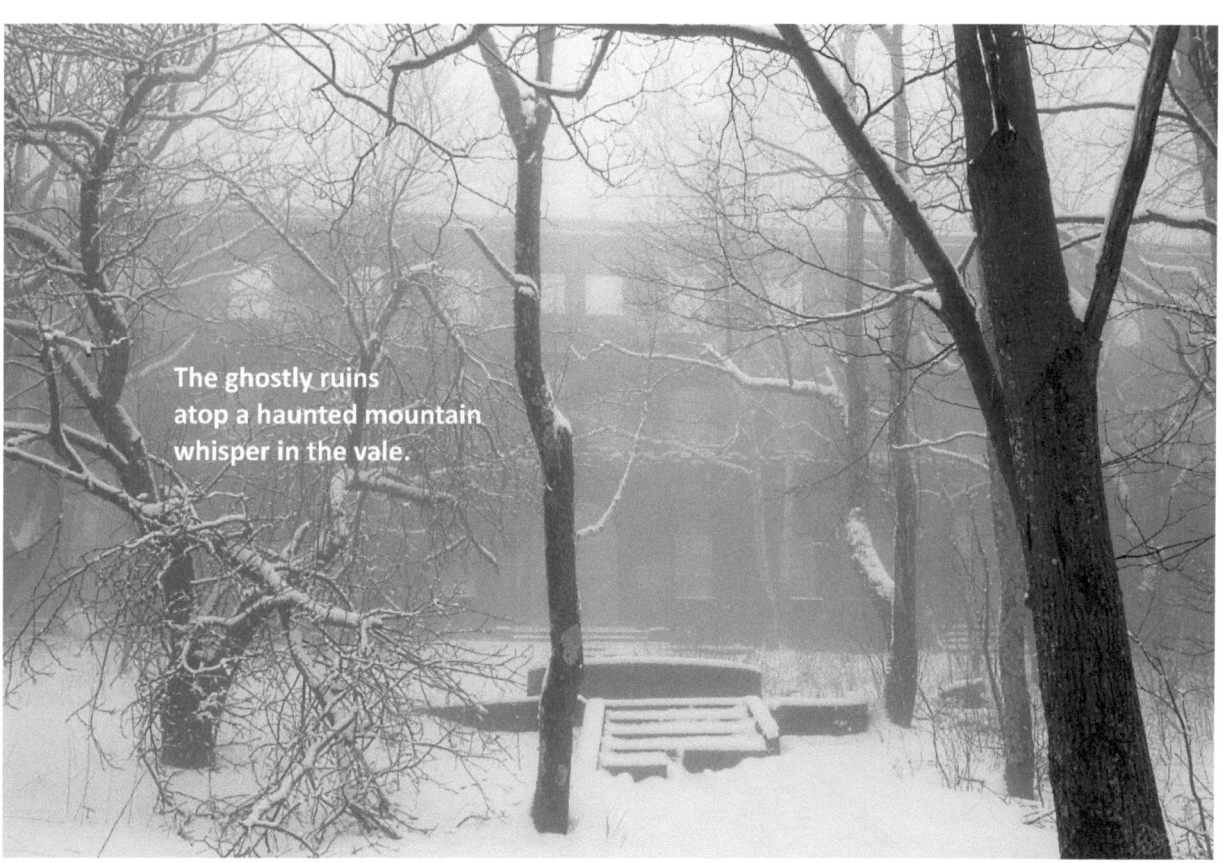

About the Author

Büg Fresh is the author of *A Thousand and One Appalachian Tales*, an account of his journey along the A.T. and through the heart of Chapel Perilous. He is also caretaker, custodian and resident flexiconographer of *The Fictionary: A vocabulous flexicon of jocu-molecular jingo and colloquialiscious flapinations in the key of G* and founder of the *International Peace Trail Project*, dedicated to the creation of "a footpath for those seeking fellowship with Earth", and to the idea that if you build it, peace will come. For more information on the IPT, please visit www.peacetrail.org. He believes humor is the missing component to world peace and has developed the formula: ☮=♥☺² ≈ Peace equals love times happiness squared. See www.biggoof.org for more.

Other books by Düg Fresh

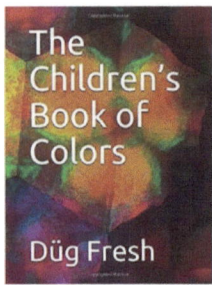

The Children's Book of Colors Paperback: A journey from primary colors to the visual spectrum and how we see – April 17, 2018   ISBN-13: 978-1980860655

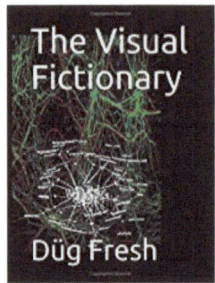

The Visual Fictionary: A vocabulous flexicon of jocu-molecular jingo and colloquialiscious flapinations in the key of G in color, visualized - Apr 10, 2018   ISBN-13: 978-1980527848

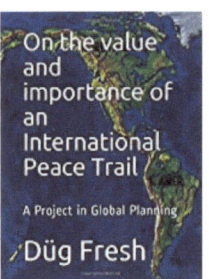

On the value and importance of an International Peace Trail: A Project in Global Planning - Mar 20, 2018   ISBN-13: 978-1980605805

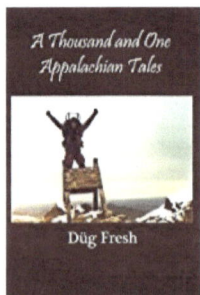

A Thousand and One Appalachian Tales: A Journey along the A.T. and through the heart of Chapel Perilous - Aug 8, 2011   ISBN-13: 978-1602648517

www.ingramcontent.com/pod-product-compliance
Lightning Source LLC
Chambersburg PA
CBHW051936210526
45473CB00006B/2267